Before I'm Dead

James Rushbrooke

methuen | drama

LONDON • NEW YORK • OXFORD • NEW DELHI • SYDNEY

METHUEN DRAMA

Bloomsbury Publishing Plc, 50 Bedford Square, London, WC1B 3DP, UK
Bloomsbury Publishing Inc, 1359 Broadway, New York, NY 10018, USA
Bloomsbury Publishing Ireland, 29 Earlsfort Terrace, Dublin 2,
D02 AY28, Ireland

BLOOMSBURY, METHUEN DRAMA and the Methuen
Drama logo are trademarks of Bloomsbury Publishing Plc.

First published in Great Britain 2026

A catalogue record for this book is available from the British Library.

Library of Congress Control Number: 2026941632

ISBN: PB: 978-1-3506-6322-0
ePDF: 978-1-3506-6323-7
eBook: 978-1-3506-6324-4

Series: Modern Plays

Typeset by Mark Heslington Ltd, Scarborough, North Yorkshire
Printed and bound in Great Britain.

For product safety related questions contact
productsafety@bloomsbury.com.

To find out more about our authors and books visit
www.bloomsbury.com and sign up for our newsletters.

Before I'm Dead
by James Rushbrooke

CAST

Zara	Myla Carmen
Stuart	Pete Ashmore

CREW

Director	Oli Savage
Producer	Eleanor Shaw
Lighting Designer	Eliska Van Lelyveld
Assistant Director	Nat Neri
Songwriter	Helen Cooper

"Brims with energy, excitement, and opportunity"
– The Guardian, 2023

VAULT Creative Arts is a multi-award-winning, internationally renowned arts company, and the previous producers of VAULT Festival – London's largest festival of performing arts. We build meaningful, low-risk opportunities for the UK's best emerging talent to grow, develop, and make ground-breaking work. We do this by creating exciting, extraordinary cultural events in unexpected locations. We breathe new life into these spaces, filling them with creativity, and inspiring audiences to fill their lives with creativity too.

THE GLITCH

The Glitch is a vibrant bar/café and unique creative space in the heart of Waterloo, created by VAULT Creative Arts. Re-launching in early 2025, the venue has developed a reputation as an intimate, exciting venue for curious audiences to see a range of brilliant comedy, music, cabaret, and special one-off events. The venue combines excellent creative output with exciting social experiences, meaning The Glitch is more than just a performance venue. It's a place to be.

The *VCA Playwriting Award* is a new initiative launched by VAULT Creative Arts. Annually, the company offers an open call for writers to submit scripts for consideration. The winning writer is awarded with a prize fee, and a four-week production of their script at The Glitch. This is just one of many things VCA does to support and develop early career artists.

Before I'm Dead is the winner of the *VCA Playwriting Award 2026*.

James Rushbrooke – Writer

James Rushbrooke is a playwright originally from Gloucester, now based in London. He writes character-driven scripts that explore big, high-concept ideas through small, interpersonal stories. Drawing on his work as a teacher and mental health advocate, his plays often focus on the psychological, ethical and moral. He believes stories should be universal, so he doesn't write for a specific audience or in a particular genre.

Shortly after moving to London in 2012, James became a writer on attachment with the Old Vic Community Company, where playwrights including Roy Williams, Morgan Lloyd Malcolm, and Kenny Emson hammered his storytelling technique into shape. This led directly to his debut play *Tomcat*, which won the 2015 Papatango Award and had a three-week run at Southwark Playhouse. *Tomcat* is currently being staged in Bucharest, where its themes of state-controlled genetics are striking a chord with new audiences.

You can find out more about him at *jamesrushbrooke.co.uk*

Oli Savage – Director

Oli Savage is an award-winning stage director, and is currently the Artistic Director and CEO of VAULT Creative Arts. He was formerly the co-founder and Artistic Director of The Greenhouse Theatre, the UK's first zero-waste theatre. His shows often involve myth, magic, storytelling and music.

Directing credits with *VCA* include:

in defence of adventurous mothers (2025) – The Glitch

The Lost Library of Leake Street (2024) – The Glitch

Directing credits with *The Greenhouse Theatre* include:

To the Ocean (2023) – The Greenhouse

Waste Age (2022) – The Design Museum

As You Like It (2021) – The Greenhouse

Swallows (2019) – The Greenhouse

The Voices we Hear (2019) – The Greenhouse

Other directing credits include:

Trump L'Oeil (2022) – Upstairs at The Gatehouse

A Midsummer Night's Dream (2018) – International Tour

Ellie Shaw – Producer

Eleanor is the Theatre Manager and in-house producer for VAULT Creative Arts. She currently specialises in producing work for basements, attics, and other unexpected locations. She's particularly interested in work that discomfits as much as it delights.

Producing credits for VAULT Creative Arts include:

in defence of adventurous mothers (2025)

The Lost Library of Leake Street (2025)

Freelance producing credits include:

medium dead (2025) – Zoo Playground

in case you thought you had no addictions, here is a list (2023) – Bush Theatre

Cast

Myla Carmen – Zara

Theatre Credits include:

Jamie Lloyd Company's Evita (West End);

Jesus Christ Superstar (UK Tour);

The Lion, The Witch and The Wardrobe (West End);

The Queen of Hearts (Greenwich Theatre)

West End Spectacular (ExCel London)

TV and Film credits include:

The Crown, Season 6 (Netflix)

The Secret Santa Project (Sea High Productions Feature Film)

Commercials include:

Lego (2023)

BP Rewards (2023)

Pete Ashmore – Stuart

Stage includes:

The Rivals, Uncle Vanya, The Circle (Orange Tree);

Romeo & Juliet (Bristol Old Vic);

Brief Encounter (SJT);

A Christmas Carol (Watermill);

Venice Preserved, The Provoked Wife (RSC);

The Lovely Bones (Birmingham Rep);

Macbeth (NT);

A Christmas Carol (Keswick);

Vernon God Little, Nothing (The Citz);

Arms and the Man (Watford Palace);

Private Lives (Mercury Theatre);

The Itinerant Music Hall (Lyric Hammersmith);

Mansfield Park (Theatre Royal Bury);

Tom's Midnight Garden (Unicorn Theatre);

Cutlery Wars (Soho Theatre);

One Snowy Night (Chichester Minerva Theatre).

Television includes:

Suspect (Disney+), *The Crown* (Netflix), *Silent Witness* (BBC), *Holby City* (BBC) and *The Bill* (ITV)

Writer's Note

Before I'm Dead was originally called *The Last Laugh* and was written directly for the VCA prize callout in late 2025/early 2026. I usually write naturalistic plays, shying away from abstract or stylised theatre out of a combination of laziness, habit and fear. So the challenge, creating a big story with just two actors, staged in the round with musical elements, really pushed me. To say I was out of my comfort zone is an understatement; at the time the first ten pages were submitted, my comfort zone was little more than a speck on the horizon.

Luckily, I share my life and home with a beautiful, talented, and extremely musical woman called Helen. She let me rifle through her back catalogue of songs to draw inspiration. This was only after I assured her the script was 'far too dark to win' and therefore it was perfectly safe to include one of her compositions. I was wrong. She is still furious with me.

The idea of a terminally ill teenager and an out-of-their-depth charity worker had been brewing for a while before I adapted it for the VCA award. I listened to Helen's song 'Missing The Moon' on repeat for a few hours, and the writing simply happened. I've worked in child protection, classrooms, and therapy-adjacent jobs for nearly two decades, so both Zara and Stuart felt familiar people to me.

For that reason, there was no planning, no structure map, no planned ending. I rarely know what will happen to my characters when I begin writing, and Zara and Stuart were no exception. They pretty much wrote themselves; I simply took the minutes and tidied up the edit. I hope you fall in love with both of them and their short-lived journey together.

I have many people to thank; for this play, for past plays, and for those plays yet to be written.

Helen, my partner in crime and creativity. Without her support I'd have gone completely insane long ago. We're fiercely independent people who are greater than the sum of our individual parts. This experiment in tolerance and continued happiness is thirteen years young and still going strong.

My Mum, for teaching me to love stories, and my Dad, for teaching me how to tell them. Being parented by a voracious reader and a raconteur was never going to end in a sensible career.

Questors Theatre in Ealing, which reminded me in a post-Covid world that there's nothing more joyful than being with like-minded creatives making imaginary worlds. Theatre is for the community and Ealing is very lucky. Every writer needs a creative home; I'm happy to call this place mine.

Emily 'Tears' Hawley, who read the first draft of this play and is always on the end of the phone when I need scriptwriting support (and ciders).

Oli, Ellie, Myla, Pete, and the whole creative team who took blueprints for an imaginary world and carefully built this world moment by moment and word by word for the rest of us to enjoy.

Kenny Emson, George Turvey, Chris Foxon, Greg and Felix Mosse, Rory Hobson, Gary Reid, Rachel Moorhead, and all the dramaturgs past and present who've helped shape my voice and hone my craft. Becoming a writer was a stupid idea, but it's brought me into contact with some truly awesome people.

Nas Patel and Tim Green, for keeping the day job bearable and full of laughs.

All the team at Methuen for creating the book you're holding and gently guiding me through the complex process of putting it there.

And lastly, thank you for coming along and supporting grass roots British theatre and a small play about unexpected connections between unlikely soulmates. This story is for everyone who has felt the icy tendrils of cancer in their life, and for those who've bravely stood beside them.

'People are people, careless in courage, but scared to the bone'

James (April 2026)

Before I'm Dead

Characters

Zara, *seventeen*
Stuart, *forty-eight*

All other characters are played by the same two actors.

Scene One

*Radio static grows to fill the space. Distortion. A flash of light.
Snap to ambient lighting.* **Zara** *blinks back into existence. She is
opposite* **Stuart** *who has a small felt puppet on his hand.*

Stuart Then when I looked at the paperwork again this
morning, I thought of course seven doesn't make a huge
amount of sense but that's what it said so . . . yeah, so I feel a
bit of a . . . Are you okay?

Zara (. . .)

Stuart Do I need to get someone?

Zara No!

Stuart You sure?

Zara I'll be fine . . . Sorry, you were saying?

Stuart About Cuddlesworth here . . .

Zara Cuddlesworth?

Stuart (*as the puppet*) Hello, I'm Cuddlesworth.

Zara Right . . .

Stuart (. . .)

Zara You're not going to use it are you?

Stuart No.

Zara Thank God . . .

Stuart It's just. Well. The paperwork was wrong you see . . .

Zara It gives strong paedo vibes is all.

Stuart *takes the puppet off his hand and reverentially puts it back
in his bag.*

Stuart Obviously he's for the younger kids.

Zara Never defend yourself in court . . . Sorry, I've missed
a few steps; who are you?

Stuart   (. . .)

Zara   Why are you looking at me like that?

Stuart   We went through . . .

Zara   Oh right . . . we already did this?

Stuart   You don't remember?

Zara *points at her head.*

Stuart (*awkwardly*)   Right . . .

Zara   You'll get used to it I'm sure . . . so you are?

Stuart   Stuart.

Zara   Zara.

She shakes his hand.

Let me guess, I already did the handshake thing?

Stuart   Yes. (*Pause.*) I have paperwork . . .

Zara   How grown up for a man with a puppet . . . You've been 'briefed'?

Stuart   A bit. I prefer . . .

Zara   You prefer to meet someone and make your own mind up about them?

Stuart   Oh, it's coming back to you?

Zara   No, just seems like something you'd say.

Stuart   I did . . .

Zara   No offence.

Stuart   Why would that be –

Zara   Because you look a bit wet.

Stuart   No offence?

Zara *shrugs. He is offended but breathes through it.*

Stuart   Would you like me to go through everything again?

Zara   Sure . . . Can we skip the bit about Mr Fucklesmuch.

Stuart   Cuddlesworth.

Zara   Whatever . . .

Stuart   So . . . Zara, seventeen not seven, following your diagnosis you've been referred to our service as an ongoing part of your therapeutic journey and my service felt we were a good match.

A long pause.

Zara   Really?

Stuart   Yes, because I mostly do the younger kids.

Zara   If the police ever get you then you should definitely do a 'no comment' interview.

Stuart   Whoever filled out the paperwork in the office filled it out wrong.

He shows her.

See? Zara Louise Russell. Female. Age. Seven. Which you're clearly not.

Zara   Clearly. They've also spelt Russell wrong.

Stuart   I was asking if you wanted to see someone else, or if you'd like to continue with me? Then you . . . you zoned out for a few seconds. (*Pause.*) Look, if you want someone else I'll have to get a new referral in, might take a few weeks.

Zara   A few weeks? Did you read the . . . no, of course you didn't. Take it from me, it's you or I'm shit out of luck.

Stuart   Right.

She points at the bag.

Zara   Not Fuckleswick though, never him.

Stuart   Great . . . I'm looking forward to it.

Zara   Me too!

Stuart   Really?

Zara   No.

Stuart   Oh.

He busies himself, gets a clipboard out. She watches him intently.

Zara   I already told the doctors what I want to do . . .

Stuart   Great. So you've got a clear idea . . .

Zara   What did they write?

Stuart   I'd prefer to hear it from you.

Zara   Straight from the horse's mouth?

Stuart   Yes . . . because people get things wrong.

Zara   Like my age?

Stuart   Exactly.

Zara   And my surname?

Stuart   Yes.

Zara   And the fact I'm not a horse?

Stuart   Huh?

Zara   Doesn't matter.

The lights flicker. **Zara** *breathes. The lights stop flickering.*

Stuart   So? What is it –

Zara   I want to do my own eulogy . . .

Stuart   Right.

Zara   Live on the radio.

Stuart   Ah.

Zara   Before I'm dead obviously.

Stuart   Good.

Zara   And it's not going to be nice . . .

Stuart   Not nice?

Zara   I'm seventeen, I've got a lot of things I want to say . . . they said I should speak to someone from your charity.

Stuart   Therapeutically?

Zara   Not much point giving me therapy is there, Stuart? Because of the –

Stuart   Of course, right, sorry –

Zara   I'm not going to die happy, I'm going to die really fucking angry and I want people on Radio 2 to hear all about it.

Stuart (*weakly*)   Radio 2?

Zara   Okay, Radio 2 might be a little bit ambitious . . . what about Severn Sound?

Stuart   Okay . . . I –

Zara   And you're going to help me.

Stuart   I can see this is something you're passionate about.

Zara   Well spotted.

Stuart   Anger is of course part of processing things –

Zara   Stuart . . . let me stop you there.

Stuart   (. . .)

Zara   I've got nothing else. I just wanted you to stop. You were about to sound like an asshole.

Stuart   I think –

Zara   Annoyingly if I was an American kid, I'd have already met John Cena or Elsa from *Frozen* by now.

Stuart   We don't have the fund –

Zara   Of course you don't because this is Cheltenham and –

Stuart   Do you want to meet Elsa from *Frozen*?

Zara   Not particularly.

Stuart   They're doing a national tour see? I think I could –

Zara   It was more of an example.

Stuart   Right. Not even Olaf?

Zara   (. . .)

Stuart   I love *Frozen*.

Zara   That makes one of us. I want to do my eulogy and I want to do my eulogy on radio.

Stuart   I don't know if I can –

Zara   What's the point of your charity then?

Stuart   We –

Zara   You grant wishes, albeit sufficiently cheap wishes like a knock-off Elsa, to terminally ill children.

Stuart   Yes.

Zara   I'm a terminally ill child, at least until February, and I'll be honest, it doesn't look good for adulthood. So I've got some things I want to say and I want to say them on a radio . . . and you can either help me or you can't.

Stuart   (. . .)

Zara   And if you'd prefer to take Mr Snugglefuck or whatever his name is and go see some five-year-old with leukaemia then that's on you . . . but I'll be doing this regardless. I've written jokes. I don't know if you know this, Stuart, but I'm actually hilarious.

Stuart   I'm getting the idea.

Zara   Good.

There is a long pause.

Stuart   I can't promise we'll get on radio.

Zara   (. . .)

Stuart   But I can promise we'll try.

There is a moment. **Zara** *breaks into a grin.*

Zara   Waheeey! That's the spirit.

Scene Two

Lights begin to turn, slow, golden, circular. The sound of a distant slightly melancholic music. A fairground, distorted by time.

Mother (*played by the actress playing* **Zara**) *sits on a bench in a large overcoat and a hat.*

Stuart *speaks in an excited childlike way.*

Stuart   The horses were the best, the ones with the flowing manes and the flared nostrils. You could drive a bus, or be on a train but I liked to be on the horses. You know where you are with horses don't you? I had a favourite one, white, and brown. Piebald I think they're called . . . I might be wrong about that. I'm not an expert on horses. My horse, Samson, he had eyes that looked angry, like he'd buck me off . . . But I knew he wouldn't. I knew because I rode him forty-three times. I counted. Round and round and round and round, the same music every time . . . I loved that music.

The music becomes more clear.

That's it.

He hums along.

And I would move up and down, up and down, and round and round in my little circle of light . . . Until.

Lights, cold, come up on the bench. **Mother** *sits staring at him.*

Stuart   A bench, wooden slats, chewing gum on the arm rest. She would sit there, sit and be watching me. Every time I came around, I would wave at her. My mother. She bought the tickets. Always five. Five rides. One after the other. She handed over the little strip of pink card and she'd say . . .

Mother (*flatly*)   Go on then.

Stuart   Go on then . . . And so I did. I rode Samson and every time he brought me round to face the bench, she was still there. She was looking, but she wasn't watching. Watching is what you do *for* someone, watching someone is being interested in their world. But my mother was just looking, looking at something, looking at nothing. Past the carousel, past the people, past Samson, past me. Somewhere else entirely.

The music wavers slightly. The lights dim.

The first few times, I waved . . . A proper big wave. Mum! Mum! Look! Mum! Look. I'd seen it on TV, children wave at their parents, their parents wave back. That's the deal, that's the circle. That's what being in the light is all about. But she never waved, she just sat. Wooden bench, chewing gum on the armrest, eyes on me but her mind elsewhere. I watched her not watching me. And my little brain, my little child brain, thought that maybe she can't see me. Maybe the carousel is too bright and she's in the dark and maybe the light is too much. I'm watching her not watching me . . . And I go round again.

He slows.

I wasn't riding for me any more, I was riding for her. To give her another chance, to give her another opportunity to look up, to see me, to wave. Just once. And every time Samson brought me round to that same cold wooden bench . . . She didn't. So, I stopped waving. I stopped watching her not watching me . . . And then we were just two people looking at each other.

The carousel lights begin to slow and the music begins to fade.

And then it would stop, I would get off . . . I would walk over to the bench and I would stand right in front of her, in front of her blocking her view of the thing that wasn't me and every time I would say . . . 'I'm done now', and she would blink . . . Like she was coming up from under some deep water and she would look at me and she would say . . .

Both   Did you have a nice time?

Stuart   And I wanted to scream at her, because if she had just watched, she would know I had a nice time . . . But because she didn't watch, I was just a stupid little boy on a stupid paint-chipped horse with angry eyes.

Mother   Did you have a nice time?

Stuart   And I said yes, because I'm seven and what else do you say? She bought the ticket, she sat on the bench, she did everything she was supposed to do. The contract between us was signed, the unspoken contract between mother and child was fulfilled.

The carousel lights fade. The low hum of the hospital returns.

Scene Three

Zara *enters.*

Stuart   There you are.

Zara   Can't get rid of me that easily.

Stuart   I was beginning to worry, I thought something had happened to you

Zara   Apart from the brain tumour?

Stuart   (. . .)

Zara   What could be worse than that?

Stuart   I don't know . . .

Zara   I needed to find something.

Stuart   What?

Zara   This.

She hands him a notebook.

These are my notes, not perfect. Not yet, but I've been working on it and I think I've got down what I want to say, but y'know . . . broad brush. What? Why are you looking at me like that?

Stuart   I have forms.

Zara   Good for you. You love forms.

Stuart   The charity wants a risk assessment . . .

Zara *laughs.*

Stuart   What?

Zara   I'm dying . . . You can't get riskier than 'will die'.

Stuart   And then there's . . . They're concerned about –

Zara   They're concerned about me saying something that will get everyone sued?

Stuart   Exactly.

Zara   Because everyone is basically a pussy these days and nobody wants to say anything bad about anyone?

Stuart *takes a large bundle of paperwork out of his bag..*

Zara   What's that?

Stuart   Broadcasting regulations.

Zara   You're kidding me?

Stuart   I had to print it off from the BBC website.

Zara   What are the broadcasting regulations?

She takes the bundle.

Stuart   There are a lot of them . . .

Zara   Give me the child-friendly version . . . I don't have long enough to live to wade through this much crap.

Stuart   Well, there's a mandatory referral required for strong language . . .

Zara   You're kidding?

Stuart   Nope.

Zara   Fuck's out?

Stuart   I'm afraid so.

Zara   Motherfucker?

Stuart   Yep.

Zara   The C-word?

Stuart   Definitely.

Zara   Then I'm going to have to seriously edit the bit about my dad. What other things am I not allowed to say?

Stuart   It leans into the whole 'generally accepted standards'.

Zara   Meaning?

Stuart   Content that is 'potentially highly offensive will need the strongest editorial justification'.

Zara   You've told them about the brain thing yeah? That's my editorial justification, tell them all about that.

Stuart   Ofcom?

Zara   Who?

Stuart   Ofcom set all these regulations . . . But no, I haven't told them. Plus, I need to complete a formal risk assessment identifying potential harm, apart from the brain tumour I mean . . . And there's privacy regulations.

Zara   If I'd known there was this much admin involved in dying, I'd have started when I was twelve.

Stuart   I'm sorry. I have to do this because impartial fairness extends to those who are discussed in context; and I have to be satisfied that you aren't coming to psychological harm as a result of this project.

Zara   I can't believe –

Stuart   It's called duty of care . . .

Zara   How long will all this take?

Stuart   I don't know but I can plough through it as best I can, and then there's this . . .

Zara (*reading*)   'Young people and vulnerable adults may not always be in a position to give informed . . .' blah blah words words words . . . 'someone over eighteen with primary responsibility for their care should normally give consent on their behalf.'

Stuart   Yep.

Zara   Does this mean my mother gets to decide?

Stuart   (. . .)

Zara   That can go in the fucking bin for starters.

Music, seductive and slightly dangerous. **Stuart** *pulls on a leather jacket.*

Scene Four

Stuart *and* **Zara** *dance.* **Zara***'s monologue can be recorded or spoken live. The punctuation of the monologue should inform the dance.*

Zara   They met at a wedding somewhere fancy, a large house in the Cotswolds. My mother was there with a boyfriend she didn't love. My father was there with a bottle of champagne he'd stolen from behind the bar. My mother smiled when she told me that. 'He had a bottle he'd stolen from behind the bar.' She said it like it was charming rather than sociopathic. Like she was in a meet-cute where the rogue turns out to have a winning smile and a heart of gold.

He was fifteen years older, had a leather jacket that smelt of cigarettes and other women. She told me once she was caught like a rabbit in headlights. She meant poetically. She meant Mills and Boon, Jane Austen, the Brontës. She forgot the rabbit usually gets hit by the truck. He thought she looked scared, which she was. Which she always was. Which he liked . . . Did I mention my father was a cu–

Stuart *spins her.*

Zara   They danced. Not nicely. Not the way that a couple should dance at a wedding. He pulled her close, too close. She let him because her boyfriend was watching. She wanted to be watched. Wanted someone, wanted everyone to see her being chosen by the man in the leather jacket who smelled of cigarettes and other women. The one everyone else admired. Admired, or avoided . . . She couldn't tell the difference. She didn't know that being chosen also meant being owned.

The way he held her . . .

She slides **Stuart**'s *hand down her back*

Zara   The hand, held low on her back, fingers pressing, was a rehearsal for ever argument, every slammed door, every raised voice, every apology she made for existing. He drank through the ceremony, through the reception, through the after-party, through the car park and then he drank through my whole childhood. By the time they tied the noose, I mean the knot, the smell of whisky with Weetabix in the morning was comfortingly familiar.

They danced at their wedding. Same song. Same grip. Same smile on his face, same fear. She told me once she should've run . . . I asked her why she didn't.

There was a long pause.

The dancing stops. **Stuart** *tries to start the dance again.*

Zars Longer.

The dancing restarts.

And then she said 'because he looked at me like I was the only person in the room'. So I told her . . . Stood there in my Christmas pyjamas with fourteen years of life behind me . . . 'That's not love.' And she laughed . . . And she told me I would find out for myself in the fullness of time and the difference between love and ownership are negligible when you're twenty-two and you're resting your head on a leather jacket.

The dance shifts tempo.

The first time he hit her, she was pregnant with me. She told him she was scared. He told her she was being dramatic. She pushed. He pushed back. She hit the kitchen counter. He said she fell, which was true but also a lie. By the time I was born, she was used to explaining away the bruises as clumsiness.

She saw the looks people gave her. The ones that said 'you chose this . . .'

And she stayed quiet because she had chosen this. She'd picked the dick in the leather jacket over the harmless boyfriend. She stared at the headlights and walked towards the car. My mother chose the man who made her feel alive in the moment, not realising until far too late that feeling alive and being slowly killed can often feel exactly the same.

And by the time she realised this, there was me. And 'you don't leave when there's a child, Zara, you stay'. You stay and your child stays with you and you tell yourself and them stories about stolen bottles of champagne and the way he held you on the dance floor.

You stay until staying is the only thing you know how to do.

Then he left anyway. Found someone else. Found someone younger. Someone who couldn't say no to the leather jacket, the smell of smoke and that winning smile.

Did I mention my dad was a . . .

Stuart *dips her. The music crescendos. The scene snaps to black.*

Scene Five

Zara *sits with a book on her lap waiting for* **Stuart** *to join her.*

Zara   C'mon, don't leave me hanging . . . what did she say?

Stuart   She said she's still reading it. She's worried you'll say something you later regret.

Zara   What later? How am I going to regret things later, there is no later.

Stuart   (. . .)

Zara   That woman has said yes to every shit offer ever presented to her. Why has she decided my future matters all of a sudden?

Stuart   I think it's quite complicated for her . . .

Zara   It isn't, it's simple. She just has to sign the form . . .

Stuart   She thinks you're angry.

Zara   She's right.

Stuart   And thinks perhaps if you were able to work through your feelings.

Zara   I don't have time to work through my feelings, I'm angry now, I've got things to say now and I want to say them before it's too late.

Stuart   Perhaps we could record some of it? Play it to her in advance . . .

Zara   I'm not going to start begging for her approval . . .

Stuart That's not what –

Zara She clocked out of my life about a decade ago, she clocked out of her life a decade before that. She's asleep at the wheel and she's only pretending to care because that's what you're supposed to do when your kid is dying.

Stuart Do you think that's fair?

Zara Yes I think that's fucking fair.

Stuart She was quite upset by –

Zara By the idea of it, sure. I'm sure she was upset by the idea of me dropping all her epically shit choices that have affected my life right into the public domain. It'll really ruin her rehearsals, you know she's auditioning to play the part of grieving mother.

Stuart (. . .)

Zara Don't be taken in by her award-winning performance. Don't you dare.

Stuart (. . .)

Zara Okay, why aren't you talking? You've always got something to say.

Stuart You seemed like you were on a roll.

Zara Don't therapy me.

Stuart I'm not.

Zara She's genuinely a shit mother and possibly an awful human being.

Stuart (. . .)

Zara What?

Stuart (*quietly*) She just seems a bit lost.

Zara She's not the one with the *fucking brain tumour*. Oh my God, I can't believe she's already made this about her and you're falling for it. I can't believe I have to spell this out for you. My mother *has to be* the centre of attention, it's part of how she's wired. This (*she points at her head*), she will dine out for years on this in her little group of friends and their silly online forum. It's a whole new tragic backstory for her . . . A new mid-season pivot in the long-running soap opera that is Annabelle Charlotte Russell. Sure, she might be losing a valuable supporting character when I die, but don't worry about her . . . she'll carry the fuck on.

She grows exasperated. The lights begin to flicker.

Stuart   Are.

Zara   A valuable supporting character.

Stuart   Are.

Zara   A valuable supplanted caricature.

Stuart   You.

Zara   A valuable caravan.

Stuart   You.

Zara   A valedictorian caveman.

Stuart   Okay?

Zara   A valley contour.

Stuart   Okay? Are you okay?

Zara *takes a breath. The lights stop flickering.*

Zara   Sorry. I'm fine . . . It doesn't like the anger.

Stuart   It?

Zara   Tumourella. Probably blood pressure.

Stuart   You sure you're okay?

Zara   I didn't mean to scare you.

Stuart   I can get someone.

Zara   No. They'll just give me drugs and make me sleep. I don't want to sleep the rest of my life away. I want to be here and living and do something.

Stuart   Okay. Good. How about we record a sample track, something light? We could play it to your mum, see how she feels about giving her consent?

Zara   Okay.

Stuart   Okay. Great. Do you need to read it?

Zara   It's my eulogy . . .

Stuart   And you know it like –

Zara   Of course I need to read it, I definitely don't want to fuck this up. It might just be the most important thing I ever have to say.

She takes out a piece of paper from her folder.

Zara   Apart from perhaps the speech I gave Ryan Pratchett in year seven about being a girl standing in front of a boy asking her to love him . . . But I stole most of that from *Notting Hill.*

Stuart   Did he notice?

Zara   About eight months later apparently, but I'd already started dating Curtis George from the year above by then. So fuck him. Ready?

Stuart   Shall I record?

Zara   Why not? You've been useless so far.

Stuart   Hey!

Zara   Sorry . . . I have to bitch a little, keeps my blood pressure low.

Stuart   As long as it's of medical value.

Zara   It certainly is (*Pause.*) You dick.

Stuart   Ready?

Zara   Ready.

The following monologue is delivered live from **Zara** *to* **Stuart**.

Zara   I arrived three weeks late, which is ironic because I'm leaving about eighty years early. The birth itself took fourteen hours, that's a full working day with additional overtime. I came out with forceps and looked like an alien. A screaming alien. I think that's fair, I'd spent nine months in a warm pool, living an expenses-paid, all-inclusive, direct room service sort of life and then I was ejected into a room full of strangers and shit fluorescent lighting. My father wasn't there, he was 'working', which I later understood meant 'being at the pub doing some racism'. My mother says she didn't mind, it gave the two of us a chance to bond. I elected not to. That felt safest. She named me Zara because it sounded exotic but fuck knows why because we lived in Cheltenham. The most exotic thing in Cheltenham is the Waitrose cheese counter. After thirty minutes of screaming, I stopped. Mum said she knew from that point I was going to be okay . . . I think I learned screaming is only a useful survival strategy if someone bothers to listen.

She trails off. Gives **Stuart** *the sign to stop the recording. He does.*

Zara   What do you think?

Stuart   I like it.

Zara   You do?

Stuart   Yeah. It's clear, it's snappy, all in all it's actually pretty good.

Zara   Thanks for the vote of confidence. I told you I'm funny.

Stuart   Have you worked it all out into bits?

Zara   A few bits, I was going to do it like chronologically . . . Bit of baby, then first day at school, some memories, then

y'know . . . some romance and stuff but I'll keep that **PG** so
Ofcom don't have a fit, and then a bit about what I'd like to
do if I wasn't dead.

Stuart   Okay.

Zara   I probably would've been prime minister or gone on
Love Island, maybe both. I'll have a think, I was so focused
on getting my GCSEs, I forgot to think about what I was
going to do with my life.

Stuart   How did they go?

Zara   I aced them . . . Oh my God, I'm going to write a bit
about how pointless exams are.

She writes in the book.

Zara   This is how eulogies work isn't it? Apart from the bit
about being in the future . . . I've never been to a funeral;
only ever seen them on TV.

Stuart   Yeah . . . You give a summary of the person's life
and you tell everyone what they were like and all the good
things about them.

Zara   Right. (*Pause.*) So I should big myself up?

Stuart   Absolutely.

Zara   Have you ever done a eulogy?

Stuart   Not my own.

Zara   No, but for like someone else.

Stuart   Yes.

Zara   (. . .)

Stuart   (. . .)

Zara   Don't leave me hanging. Who?

Stuart   My mother.

Zara   Oh.

Stuart   Yeah.

Zara   That sucks.

Stuart   Oh yeah.

Zara   Was it really depressing?

Stuart   They usually are . . .

Zara   Were you close?

Stuart   Sometimes.

Zara   How old were you when –

Stuart   Seventeen.

Zara   Oh. Wait . . . Snap. I mean my mum is fine, but we're both doing a eulogy at seventeen. What are the chances?

Stuart   Low.

He shifts uncomfortably.

Sorry . . .

Zara   How did she die?

Stuart   (. . .)

Zara   I don't have a filter, because of my brain . . . Actually that's not true, I'm just nosy and stuff.

Stuart   It's all right. She killed herself.

Zara   Shit. You want me to get Captain Snorkelbork? You could chat about your feelings and shit.

Stuart   Ha!

Zara   Yeah . . . See how much it sucks from this side?

Stuart   I guess so.

Zara   Do you think Mr Bumblefuck could be a cloth manifestation of your own grief?

Stuart   Who knows?

Zara   Me. I did GCSE Psychology last year, which absolutely nobody has ever mentioned since . . . I think Mr . . . what is his actual name?

Stuart   Cuddlesworth.

Zara   Mr Cuddlesworth is a manifestation of your own unprocessed grief . . .

Stuart   It's not actually Mr Cuddlesworth. It's just Cuddlesworth.

Zara   Non-binary? That's very modern for a man who wears M&S shirts.

Stuart   Leaves space for the kids to put their own interpretation on it . . .

Zara   I see.

Stuart   Plus there's the song.

Zara   There's a song?

Stuart   Yes.

Zara   There's. A. Song?!

Stuart   Yes.

Zara   Okay. Sing me the song.

Stuart   I don't have my guitar.

Zara   Wait. What? You play guitar?

Stuart   Yes.

Zara   Okay, we'll circle back to that, there's a lot I don't know about you. Sing me the song.

Stuart   No.

Zara   Sing me the song. A cappella.

Stuart   Absolutely not.

Zara   I have a brain tumour and it's my dying wish to hear the Cuddlesworth song. You cannot deprive a dying girl of her right to hear the best song in the world sung by a puppet . . . The puppet sings it right?

Stuart   Yes.

Zara   This is brilliant. Sing me the song.

Stuart   I –

Zara (*firmly*)   Dying wish.

Stuart *sings. He is somewhere between embarrassed, self-aware and amused.* **Zara** *tries (and fails) to hide her amusement.*

Stuart
When you're feeling sad and blue
And you don't know what to do.
Just remember, can't you see.
That cuddles are the key.
Cuddlesworth! Cuddlesworth!
Always worth it, that's my curse
Give me a squeeze and so you'll see . . .
Cuddlesworth is the one for me.

Zara *applauds.*

Zara   Please tell me there's a second verse?

Stuart   Just the one.

Zara   Is that because the kids have died? Choked themselves out on their own IV drips? Thrown themselves out of windows?

Stuart   I sometimes repeat it.

Zara (*nodding solemnly*)   Good. Finish them off . . .

Stuart   Hey, you survived.

Zara   Barely. (*Pause.*) For what it's worth, you have a nice voice.

Stuart   Thanks.

Scene Six

Stuart *sits alone with his guitar case. The sound of the merry-go-round and colourful lights fill the space. The merry-go-round gets faster and more intense.*

Zara *enters and sits beside him. They don't talk. She puts her hand on his. The merry-go-round slows and eventually stops. He smiles at her.*

The following monologue is played as a recording and acted out by **Zara** *and* **Stuart.**

Zara   My earliest memory is our holiday. It was the only one we ever went on as a family so that's why it sticks in my brain, like an anti-tumour . . . My mother still talks about it like it's a miracle, which given how much money we didn't have, and what a shit my dad was, isn't far wrong. We went to a shabby caravan park in Weston-super-Mare, which is not, as destinations go, anything like the Maldives. But I was five years old and I didn't know the difference, couldn't have pointed to the Maldives on a map. Still can't. To little me, a caravan was a magic box on wheels, the sea was a giant brown puddle, and the amusement arcades were little temples of glittering lights and intoxicating sounds where you could win small toys if you were very very lucky.

And I was very very lucky.

I won five pink, green and blue plastic dinosaurs and I called them all Timothy, which was my favourite name for some reason. My father came down a day later, drove separately. Mum pretended this was 'because of work' but was probably because he couldn't bear to be in the car with us for the hour-and-a-half journey down the M5.

He arrived, looked at the caravan, decided it was cosy and fucked off to the pub.

He came back at closing time, woke everyone up getting into the caravan and then getting into bed. Then he came to the beach the next day with sunglasses on and didn't speak to anyone. On the second day, just before he left . . . he took me on the donkeys. Just me. He put me on this sad-looking grey donkey called Trevor and walked beside me for ten minutes. Maybe a little longer. And for a bit he was just my dad. A normal dad like the other kids had. Holding the rope, telling me to hold on and be careful, smiling when I laughed and keeping me steady.

Maybe it was guilt. Maybe it was for the photo-op, everyone loves a donkey after all . . . But I remember the way his hand looked on the rope. His hands were dirty, his fingernails were long. I remember him saying 'good girl' when I got off Trevor without complaining and we got a lolly from a shop on the waterfront. He left that evening after a blazing row with my mum. Gone before tea time. My mother cried in the caravan while I played with the Timothys on the little patch of grass outside and thought about the fact my dad had nice hands.

That's my first memory. Ten minutes on a donkey with a man who'd go on to forget my birthday six months later.

We transition back to live, **Zara** *speaks directly to* **Stuart***.*

And that's the thing about children, we're all so stupid. We'll take anything offered to us, a scrap, a crumb of love, ten minutes on a donkey and we'll call it 'enough' because that's what enough feels like when you're five and you're playing with dinosaurs over the sound of sobbing.

A long pause.

Stuart   I think you did that one perfectly?

Zara   You do?

Stuart   I do . . .

Zara   Anything from Mum?

Stuart   She's a hard no.

Zara   Did you play her the –

Stuart   Some of it.

Zara   Did you play her the first bit?

Stuart   Yes.

Zara   She still said no?

Stuart   She still said she won't sign.

Zara   Figures.

Stuart   So . . .

Zara   Did you see it yet?

Stuart   (. . .)

Zara   Yeah you did . . . You saw it.

Stuart   Maybe you could –

Zara   You get it now, don't you. It's all about her isn't it? It's always about her.

Stuart   (. . .)

Zara   Oh I forgot, you've got to be professional and shit . . . But take my word for it, this, all of this, will always all be about her. Fuck her. I think we should do it anyway, I've seen *Shawshank Redemption*. We could do a pirate broadcast..

Stuart   There might be another way.

Zara   How?

Stuart   Parental consent.

Zara   I know what parental consent means, and she said no.

Stuart   Parental consent, not Mum's consent.

Zara   Oh fuck no. I haven't spoken to him in years . . . I know we agreed not to use the C-word, but even thinking about him brings it to the tip of my tongue.

Stuart   I'm just letting you know the law.

Zara   Cu . . . Cu . . . Cu . . . Considering what a twat he is, I'd rather do the pirate broadcast.

Stuart   It's up to you.

Zara   You think I should?

Stuart   I'm not saying anything, I'm making you aware of options.

Zara   It's not really an option.

Stuart   Then we're stuck.

Zara   I suppose.

Stuart   Nothing to lose.

Zara   Is that a brain cancer joke?

Stuart   No!

Zara   I'm teasing. (*Pause.*) Did you bring your guitar?

Stuart   It's in the car.

Zara   Go get it then.

Stuart   I'm –

Zara   Go. And. Get. It.

Stuart *exits.* **Zara** *smiles. The static begins, louder, echoing, the pressure builds. She holds her head trying to dislodge the sound. It grows, continues to build. She moves to the floor and presses her head against the floor.*

She stays this way for some time. The pressure continues to build.

Stuart *enters with a guitar case.*

Stuart   Zara?!

Snap blackout.

Scene Seven

Zara *and* **Stuart** *sit in front of two mannequins covered in costumes. The following scene is played chaotically with them swapping between characters, playing each other's characters, using the mannequins as characters.*

Zara   Okay . . . Explain it to me again.

Stuart   Right.

He takes a deep breath.

Your mother emailed the office, she said . . .

Mother   Dear sir or madam. I am writing to complain about the conduct of one of your staff, Stuart Harrison. I have become very concerned about his relationship with my daughter Zara Louise Russell . . .

Zara   What a bitch.

Stuart   So then she called a meeting.

Mother   Thank you for taking the time to meet with me.

Worker One   No problem at all, Mrs Russell, we wanted to assure you that we take all child protection concerns very seriously.

Worker Two   Very seriously.

Worker One   Now we understand your daughter Sarah.

Mother   Zara.

Worker Two   Your daughter Zara. We're taking this very seriously by the way . . .

Worker One   Your daughter Zara may have struck up an inappropriate relationship with one of our staff members?

Worker Two   And Sarah.

Worker One   Zara.

Both   We're taking this very seriously.

Mother   Stuart Harrison. He has been giving my daughter therapy . . .

Worker One   Stuart is one of our more experienced therapists.

Worker Two   Very experienced.

Mother   Working with her on a project.

Worker One   A project?

Worker Two   What sort of project?

Mother   She wants to broadcast her own eulogy.

Worker Two   We need to take that very seriously.

Worker One   Broadcast her own eulogy?

Worker Two   It says here she's seven.

Mother   She's seventeen.

Worker One   Oh . . .

Worker Two   Oh . . .

Mother   Is that a problem?

Worker One   We're project managers for the under-twelve cohort.

Worker Two   And Sarah.

Worker One   Zara.

Worker Two   Zara. Sorry. She is over twelve.

Worker One   She's five years over twelve.

Worker Two   You're going to need to speak with Sinead.

Mother   Sinead?

Worker One   Yes, Sinead. She manages the team that deals with the over-twelves.

Mother   Fine. How do I get hold of Sinead?

Sinead   I'm Sinead. How can I help?

Mother   I'd like to raise some concerns about my daughter.

Sinead   Is she over twelve?

Mother   Seventeen.

Sinead   Then you've come to the right place. I'm Sinead. I manage the over-twelves.

Mother   I know.

Sinead   So what are your concerns?

Mother   About Stuart Harrison.

Sinead   Stuart Harrison? From the under-twelves team? Funny-looking man? Creepy puppet. He works for the under-twelves team. You need to speak to Biggins and Bilbo.

Mother   I already spoke to Biggins and Bilbo . . .

Zara   Tell me they weren't actually called Biggins and Bilbo?

Stuart   No. They're called Christina Biggs and David Martin.

Zara   So why are they . . .

Worker One   Chrissie Biggins, I have a coffee cup which says 'You don't have to be mad to work here, but it helps'.

Worker Two   David Martin. I paint tiny figurines of elves for fun, I have a miniature Lothlórien in my garage, it's located just east of the misty mountains and just beyond the tyre pressure checker.

Stuart   We are getting way off-track.

Zara   Sorry. I like the details.

Mother   Stuart Harrison . . . has actively encouraged my daughter to get in contact with her father and she'll be looking to cut me out of the eulogy.

Sinead   Out of the eulogy?

Mother   Yes.

Sinead   Whose eulogy?

Mother   Zara's eulogy.

Sinead   Zara's dead? Jesus Christ. In that case we must take things VERY seriously.

Mother   No. She isn't dead . . . She is writing her own eulogy, which she wants to broadcast on radio . . . And Stuart Harrison has gone behind my back to make it happen.

Sinead   Ah, I see . . . Well, leave this with me. Me, I'm Sinead from the over-twelves after all.

Mother   I expect something to happen.

Sinead   Something will happen. Something will definitely happen. What would you like to happen?

Mother   I want Stuart Harrison to be fired for gross misconduct.

Sinead   We take that very seriously.

Zara   Wait, she actually wants you fired?

Stuart   She wants me fired.

Zara   The bitch.

Stuart   So then there was a meeting.

Sinead   Stuart . . . Thanks for coming in.

Stuart   No worries.

Sinead   There have been some concerns.

Worker One   We have concerns.

Sinead   About your working relationship with Zara.

Stuart   Right.

Sinead   There's been a complaint, from Zara's mother.

Stuart   Okay.

Sinead   She has concerns about the project.

Stuart   I know she does.

Sinead   And we're taking this very seriously.

Worker One   Very seriously indeed. David?

There is a long pause.

Worker Two   Sorry . . . I'm actually off on leave by this point. I'm hand painting a Balrog to go in the downstairs bathroom.

Sinead   We'd like to get to the bottom of the complaint.

Stuart   Zara has a clear idea of what she wants.

Sinead   Something you've encouraged her to do?

Stuart   That's what she wanted

Sinead   Wouldn't she like to meet an Elsa?

Stuart   No.

Sinead   What about Olaf?

Stuart   Writing and recording her own eulogy are the instructions she's given me. It's helping her process what's happening, it's good for her to get closure. That's obviously what we want.

Sinead   Obviously.

Stuart   And so . . .

Sinead   And so you got hold of her father via social media, explained everything in detail to him, coordinated a direct meeting between the two of them and threw caution to the wind. Dammit Stuart, what the hell are you playing at?

Stuart   I –

Sinead   This is a blatant and total disregard for all the policies and procedures we have in place, not to mention all the policies we have, and the procedures that are in place. Policies and procedures, Stuart, policies and procedures goddammit, man, you're a reckless buffoon playing fast and loose with what are established policedures.

Stuart   You're over-egging it slightly, that's not what happened.

Zara   I know because I messaged him myself.

Stuart   Yes you did.

Sinead   So, Stuart Harrison, what do you have to say for yourself now that we've upheld Mrs Russell's complaint and you've been instructed to drop the project.

Stuart   You're wrong.

Sinead   What about the policies and procedures. And before you answer, can I remind you, we're taking this very seriously.

Stuart   So am I. All I did was remind her that she has two parents, not one . . . And that either parent could grant her permission to broadcast her eulogy.

Zara   And what did she say?

Stuart   I don't know . . .

Sinead   Mr Harrison, we have very clear policies and procedures around complaints and if you . . .

Stuart *takes a name-badge or tie off.*

Sinead   What are you doing?

Zara   Wait . . . You walked out? Stuart . . . You walked out?!

Stuart   Yes.

Zara   You walked out of your job?

Stuart   Yes.

Zara   For me?

Stuart   Yes.

There's a beat.

Zara   Aren't you worried . . .

Stuart   No.

Zara   Can't you get your job back?

Stuart   I doubt it . . . I told David he could shove his Balrog up his ass.

Zara *laughs.*

Blackout.

Scene Eight

Stuart, *as* **Zara***'s father, sits in a leather jacket.*

Father   Your mother tells it different, she remembers it different too. Your mother only remembers what she wants to remember and she's good at that, boy is she good at that. Sorry. I'm rambling . . . But your message took me by surprise. I remember a woman by the fire exit trying not to cry because her boyfriend was ignoring her. I felt for her . . . So I walked over with a bottle of red from the table . . . It wasn't champagne and I didn't steal it. The wine was free during the lunch, but nobody on my table drank red, so I walked over, gave her bottle and said something stupid like, 'Looks like you need this more than me.'

She laughed. I laughed. That's the whole thing.

And yeah, we danced . . . We were both looking for something and because people are stupid, even older people like me . . . we were looking in the wrong places. Neither of us found what we were looking for, but she needs the version of me that was a monster . . . It's the only way everything makes sense to her; the only way nothing is her fault . . . so that's the version of me she kept.

That's the version of me she's given you.

Lights up to reveal **Zara** *in a hospital bed listening to this on her mobile phone.*

Father   I'm not perfect, God knows I'm not. (*Pause.*) I've been sober for four years now . . . Not that it matters. You don't get bonus points for fixing up the house after you've already knocked it down. The day I left, we fought and it was a real doozy . . . Your mother and me, screaming at each other like we were the last two people on earth, no regard for anyone. It was the sort of fight where you can't take things back . . . I walked out mid-sentence and left her shouting and crying to empty air. I picked you up from school and I took you to the playground near the bookies, the one where the swings always squeaked. You played. I watched. I didn't tell you. I couldn't, you were far too busy and you were happy.

You fell asleep in the car on the way home. And I sat there for twenty minutes, before I texted your mother.

She brought out all my stuff . . . One suitcase. That's how little of me was left in the house . . . And she said 'Are you going to tell her?' and I shook my head. She told me she'd tell you something . . . So she did, she told you I'd found someone else, but that wasn't true. That night, I just drove around for hours, ended up in a Tesco car park in Tewkesbury. I thought about going back, I thought about you waking up the next morning and me not being there . . . It was a few weeks ahead of your birthday, I sent a card, I sent some money . . . I never heard anything more.

She wasn't wrong to want me gone, God knows I'd given her plenty of reasons over the years, but it was a two-way street. I used to sit in pubs, that's before I stopped going to pubs, and I'd wonder what you were doing. I used to wonder whether you'd inherited my sense of fun, my joy for life, or your mother's sense of victimhood.

I played your recordings. I played your recordings and I sat in my shitty one-bed flat and I laughed . . . You got it. You got my side. You're seventeen, you're dying, and you're still funny.

I remember Trevor the donkey; you picked the sad one because you said he was sad and never got picked because he was scruffy. That was you aged five with your infectious grin, always trying to make sad things happy. I don't know if that's still you, probably not, no amount of energy would ever make your mother happy.

God knows, I gave up trying.

You said you need a signature . . . I'll sign. Whatever you need. You don't have to see me and you sure as hell don't have to talk to me if you don't want to. If I'm in your eulogy, I'm in it as the villain. That's fair. I earned that. I'm not going to say I'm proud of you . . . That's what people say when they want to feel better about themselves and the shitty things they've done and god knows I don't get to feel better.

Whatever you need, let me know. I'm sorry that it's too little, too late.

Zara *puts her phone under her pillow, puts her pillow over her face.*

Snap blackout.

Scene Nine

Zara *is in a hospital bed. The static returns. Over the top the voicemail plays.*

Voicemail   I'm not going to say I'm proud of you . . . That's what people say when they want to feel better and God knows I don't get to feel better. Whatever you need, let me know. I'm sorry it's too little, too late.

Stuart *enters with a case. She plays the last bit of the voicemail.*

Voicemail   Whatever you need, let me know. I'm sorry it's too little, too late.

Stuart   You okay?

Zara   (. . .)

Stuart   The doctors said you'd had an episode, said you were resting.

Zara   (. . .)

Stuart   I can come back.

Zara   No.

Stuart   If you're not up to it . . .

Zara   I'm good, just tired is all.

Stuart   Okay.

He comes to sit next to her. There is silence for a while.

Your father sent back the forms.

Zara   Yes.

Stuart   The project is a go; did you work out an ending? Think about your career choices?

Zara *shakes her head.*

Stuart   Did you want to re-record what we already did? Maybe at higher quality. I've brought a microphone. (*Pause.*) I've also provisionally made contact with Radio 2.

Zara   Radio 2? What?

Stuart   I was . . . I thought, maybe, if I pitched it right . . . This would be a really good 'pause for thought'.

Zara   What the fuck is 'Pause for Thought'?

Stuart   It's like a little religious bit during the morning, someone wise comes on, dispenses a bit of wisdom . . . Gives everyone 'Pause for Thought'.

Zara   And people listen to this?

Stuart   Lots of people, yeah.

Zara   Wow.

Stuart   They said they might consider it, subject to content, etc. . . . But they were very intrigued about it. Intrigued about what you wanted to say, what insights you wanted to share . . . The woman on the phone sounded like she was going to cry.

Zara   Wahey.

Stuart   Wahey indeed. So, I'm all yours for the next hour. How do you want to tackle it?

A long pause.

Zara   I don't.

Stuart   I should come back when you –

Zara   I don't want to do a eulogy.

Stuart   (. . .)

Zara   Sorry.

Stuart   No, it's just that –

Zara   It was a bad idea.

Stuart   It wasn't.

Zara   It was.

Stuart   You're allowed to change your mind.

Zara   Don't be a dick.

Stuart   (. . .)

Zara   You can be angry at me. You can shout at me.

Stuart   Why would I be angry with you?

Zara   Messing you around.

Stuart   You haven't messed me around?

Zara   You walked out on the charity . . .

Stuart   Because they didn't take me seriously, which means they weren't taking you seriously. Which violated my principles . . . you can't work for a charity that says it wants to put the children at the centre of everything they do, but doesn't.

Zara   But what about your, who's going to feed Cuddlesworth?

Stuart   One of the few benefits of dying young is that you'll never have to meet anyone from a HR department. Even if the charity wanted to fire me tomorrow, they'd still have to go through a twelve-week process, I'd have to be interviewed sixteen times, I'd get a union rep, this could tie them up for years. They'll have to pay me a fortune to leave with the level of incompetency they've got going on.

Zara   Good

Stuart   So in the meantime, I'm officially 'on gardening leave'.

Zara   You're gardening?

Stuart   I live in a flat, so no. It means I get paid for staying at home.

Zara   Wahey!

Stuart   Wahey indeed.

Zara   (. . .)

Stuart   How come you don't want to do a eulogy anymore?

Zara   I dunno.

Stuart   You don't want to say anything on the record.

Zara   It's not that.

Stuart   No?

Zara   I was angry . . . Now I'm not. I tried writing some funny stuff this morning, it all came out shit.

Stuart   You can't be funny all the time.

Zara   I've always been funny, it's my thing.

Stuart   What did you write about?

Zara   I tried to write about actual dying.

Stuart   The funniest of all the funny subjects.

Zara   Yeah.

Stuart   So, what have you got?

Zara   Not very far.

She pushes her notebook towards him. He reads it. The words 'I'm scared' are projected all over the performing space.

A beat. He hugs her. She doesn't resist. After a while he hums the Cuddesworth tune. She laughs.

Zara   Why do you have to ruin everything?

Stuart   Sorry.

Zara   I'm being silly. I'm not actually scared.

Stuart   You are . . . And that's okay.

Zara   Do the song again.

Stuart (*singing*)
   When you're feeling sad and blue

Zara   For the love of fuck just hum it.

He does.

Blackout.

Scene Ten

The sound of the merry-go-round and colourful lights fill the space, though the tune is much more familiar – it's the Cuddlesworth song.

Stuart *sits on the bench and watches for a while.*

Zara *enters. Much younger. She's got a fish in a bag and a lolly. They watch each other for a while.*

Zara   What are you watching for?

Stuart   Someone. You?

Zara   Just showing my fish around.

Stuart   It's a piece of carrot.

Zara   You're a piece of carrot. How long have you been here?

Stuart   As long as I can remember.

Zara   What are you watching for?

Stuart   Just someone.

She stares in the same direction as him.

Zara   There's nobody there.

Stuart   I know.

Zara   You've lost somebody.

Stuart   No, they just haven't arrived yet.

Zara *sighs and sits on the bench.*

Zara   Sit. (*Pause.*) Say hello to the fish.

Stuart   Hello, fish.

Zara   Do you want some lolly?

Stuart   No thank you.

They wait a little longer.

Zara   A merry-go-round without people is just horses.

Stuart   Yeah.

Zara   And horses without riders get what is called 'disqualified'.

A beat.

Stuart   What?

Zara   My dad taught me that, at the library.

Stuart   The library?

Zara   Maybe not the library, somewhere with books.

Stuart   The bookies?

Zara   Yeah. I always picked the fastest horse but they were only the fastest because nobody was sitting on them . . . And a merry-go-round with nobody on it is just noise and machinery.

Stuart   Yeah.

Zara   And it's worse than that, the horses just go round and round and round forever.

Stuart   (. . .)

Zara   And they don't get anywhere.

Stuart   (. . .)

Zara   When you're up there, you do at least feel like you're getting somewhere . . . Even if you are actually just coming back to where you started.

Stuart   True.

Zara   So why are we still on the bench?

Stuart   Habit.

Zara   I'm going on the horses.

Stuart   You'll fall off . . .

Zara   So?

Stuart   You'll hurt yourself.

Zara   So?

Stuart   You'll . . .

Zara   I'll what?

Stuart   I don't know.

Zara   Exactly. I'll ride the horses and you watch me in case I fall off.

Stuart   Okay.

Zara   Which I won't.

Stuart   Okay.

Zara   And even if I do, that's okay.

Stuart   Which one are you going to ride?

Zara   The white and brown one.

Stuart   (. . .)

Zara   He has the best eyes. Are you coming?

Stuart   I'll sit here. I'll watch.

Zara   Will you actually watch?

Stuart   I don't know. I don't think I'd be very good. I think you'd probably just go round and round and I'd sit here . . . And the whole thing would begin again.

Zara   The whole thing?

Stuart   The merry-go-round. Five times. Five tickets. Five chances.

Zara   You're good at seeing people.

Stuart   I've had a lot of practice.

Zara   Yeah. Okay . . . Watch.

The music starts up and **Zara** *enters the merry-go-round. She waves at* **Stuart**.

He waves back. He smiles. He watches her. She gets off.

Stuart   Did you have a nice time?

Zara   Sure.

Stuart   Did you have a nice time?

Zara   Does it matter?

Stuart   Did you have a nice time?

Zara   I'm not going to answer that question.

Stuart   Did you have a nice time?

Zara   Here's the thing. Hold my fish. If I had a nice time, you should've seen. If I didn't have a nice time, you should've seen. The question isn't important.

Stuart   (. . .)

Zara   So, I could say yes . . . But I'd be lying.

Stuart   Did you –

Zara   It was a bit shit after the first go . . . But I liked that you liked it.

Stuart   How . . .

Zara   Because I watched you enjoy it.

Blackout.

Scene Eleven

Zara *sits on the bed. The sound of static is intermittent through this scene.*

Stuart   So . . . I didn't bring any equipment, I just brought the guitar like you asked. How are you feeling?

Zara   Better. A lot better.

Stuart (*sadly*)   Good.

He unpacks the guitar and gives it to her. She strums a little.

Stuart   I've got a capo if you need one?

She continues to strum underneath the rest of this scene.

Stuart   What do you want to talk about? Have you come up with an alternative to your eulogy idea?

Zara   No.

Stuart   Your dad got in contact with me, he wants to know if he should come and see you.

Zara   If he has to check, then no.

Stuart   He said you're not replying to his messages.

Zara   No.

Stuart   Your mum dropped her complaint.

Zara   Good.

Stuart   What's that you're playing?

Zara   Metallica.

Stuart   Really? I didn't think kids your age knew Metallica.

Zara   I'm seventeen, not dead.

Stuart   So . . . What shall we talk about?

Zara *shrugs.*

Stuart   You want me to go?

Zara   No.

Stuart   Okay . . .

The static starts to cut in.

Zara   You.

Stuart Me?

Zara Yes.

Stuart I'm not supposed to talk about me. It's not really the done –

Zara Who am I going to tell?

Stuart You've got a point.

Zara If you've got any secrets, don't worry I'll take them to my grave.

Stuart What do you want to know?

Zara What are you going to do after?

Stuart After?

Zara *shrugs.*

Stuart Oh, after-after . . . I don't know. I could get a new job I suppose.

Zara You should join a band.

Stuart Right.

Zara You and Cuddlesworth could rock the O2.

Stuart We could.

Zara *takes a small card out of her book and hands it to* **Stuart**.

Stuart What's this?

Zara An invitation.

Stuart To . . .

Zara It's my official invitation, will you come to my funeral?

Stuart Do you want me to?

Zara I won't care, I'll be dead. And you've got an invitation written and signed by me in case my mum tries to throw you out. Does she hate you? Will she try and throw you out?

Stuart   Maybe.

Zara   You should let Cuddlesworth do the eulogy.

Stuart   That can be the final nail in my career as a therapist.

Zara   And then let him hammer the final nail in my actual coffin.

Stuart   He doesn't have hands.

Zara   Poor bastard, how does he feel?

Stuart   Funny.

Zara   Always. You can bring someone if you like?

Stuart   Ah.

Zara   Apart from Cuddlesworth . . . He'll get his own invitation, a little one. Probably in gold pen.

Stuart   I haven't got anyone to bring.

Zara   You're not married?

Stuart   No.

Zara   Dating?

Stuart   Not for a while.

Zara   Why not?

Stuart   Haven't felt the need.

Zara   That puppet is holding you back.

Stuart   He probably is.

Zara   Tell me he's not on your Tinder profile.

Stuart   I don't have a Tinder profile.

Zara   More of a Bumble man?

Stuart   (. . .)

Zara   You're wet.

They listen to **Zara** *play music for a while. She's picking out a new tune.*

Stuart   I like that. What's the tune?

Zara   I don't know, just making it up.

Stuart   You –

Zara   If I wasn't going to be prime minister or go on *Love Island*, I'd probably headline Glastonbury.

Stuart   I'm sure you would.

Zara   You should get married.

Stuart *laughs.*

Stuart   It's not that easy.

Zara   You should get married and have kids.

Stuart   Okay.

Zara   Don't just say okay and then not do it. There are so many shit parents in the world, take that from me . . . You'd be good. Get married and have kids. Promise me.

Stuart   I don't make promises.

Zara   Why not?

Stuart   Therapy code of conduct.

Zara   Killjoy. You've got to get out in the dating scene.

Stuart   I'll try.

Zara   Do you have any girlfriends? (*Pause.*) Friends that are girls?

Stuart   A few.

Zara   Get them to pick your shirts in future . . .

Stuart   Seems like a good plan . . .

Zara   And in this notebook are a list of places I wanted to visit. You have to visit them all . . .

Stuart   I'll –

Zara   One of them is the moon.

Stuart   Okay . . .

Zara   And when you get married.

Stuart   If –

Zara   When you get married, you have to have at least two children.

Stuart   Okay . . . Why at least two.

Zara   Only children are weird; I'm an only child.

Stuart   Noted.

Zara   And if you don't have children and you don't get past the whole shirt and puppet thing, then you have to adopt.

Stuart   I have to?

Zara   Yes. And name them both Zara, after me.

Stuart   What if I have a boy?

Zara   Still Zara.

Stuart   Seems harsh.

Zara   Not my problem, I'll be dead.

Stuart   Terrifying.

They listen to the music for a while.

Zara   How many kids did you do this for?

Stuart   Do what for?

Zara   Therapy stuff.

Stuart   Nine. You're my ninth.

Zara   Am I your favourite?

Stuart   (. . .)

Zara   You have to say yes.

Stuart   (. . .)

Zara   All the others are dead. Wait. They are all dead aren't they?

Stuart   Yes.

They listen to the music for a while.

Zara   Any of them haunt you?

Stuart   Not yet.

Zara   I can be the first. Did you go to their funerals?

Stuart   Some of them. It depends.

Zara   I'm not scared any more.

Stuart   I'm glad.

Zara   I've started writing again.

Stuart   Jokes?

Zara   Poems.

Stuart   Poems? That's new.

Zara   I've always written poems, but you have to keep some things to yourself.

Stuart   Yes you do.

Zara   I'm going to ask you a question and I really want you to think before you answer.

Stuart   Okay . . .

Zara   What does it mean that I'm feeling better?

Stuart   (. . .)

Zara I feel much better today –

Stuart It's called terminal lucidity.

Zara (. . .)

Stuart It's when –

Zara I know. I already googled it.

Stuart Why ask me then?

Zara I wanted to see if you'd tell me, the doctors won't.

Stuart (. . .)

Zara You don't lie?

Stuart No.

Zara The other kids, were they as angry as me?

Stuart No. Scared mostly.

Zara I'm not scared anymore.

Stuart No?

Zara No, that's a lie. I'm sorry.

Stuart People fluctuate . . . Children, adults, it's not like there's one way to do this. It's not like I've ever done it . . .

Beat.

Zara You're really good at your job.

Stuart Thanks.

Zara I have something for you

Stuart Oh.

She takes out a book from beneath her pillow.

Zara Poems.

Stuart (. . .)

Zara Read one of these. You can choose . . .

Stuart   (. . .)

Zara   Do *not* let Cuddlesworth do any of them.

Stuart *laughs. He takes the book.*

Zara   I'm tired.

She gives him the guitar. The static subsides for a second.

Stuart   I'll let you get some sleep.

Zara   Thanks for coming.

Stuart   You're welcome.

He goes to leave.

Zara   Stuart?

Stuart   Yes.

Zara   Thanks for everything.

Stuart   You're welcome.

The static grows.

Scene Twelve

Stuart *stands with his guitar next to the empty bed.*

Radio Host   And now we've got something a little different today on Radio 2. Stuart Harrison . . .

Stuart   Hello.

Radio Host   So, you're a therapist from London who was working closely with a young girl called Zara.

Stuart   Zara Russell, yes.

Radio Host   She's sadly no longer with us . . .

Stuart   No . . . She died two years ago, 19 February at four in the morning, just shy of her eighteenth birthday.

Radio Host   And I understand, she left you with strict instructions . . .

Stuart   Yes. Zara was determined to do her own eulogy.

Radio Host   But sadly, you couldn't make that happen in time?

Stuart   No. And she asked me to read a poem at her funeral.

Radio Host   And you didn't manage that?

Stuart   No, for complicated reasons that I won't go into, that didn't happen.

Radio Host   I'm sorry to hear that.

Stuart   Life, and sometimes death, gets in the way of the best-laid plans.

Radio Host   And I understand that Zara left you with a long to-do list?

Stuart   She did . . . A list of places to visit. A list of things to see.

Radio Host   A bucket list?

Stuart   Yes.

Radio Host   Well . . . That must be difficult.

Stuart   Sometimes.

Radio Host   I bet she would've loved this?

Stuart   Oh absolutely, she would've had some things to say.

Radio Host   Why don't you tell us why you got in touch after two years?

Stuart   I was talking about Zara with my partner David, we both love music and I showed him some of the poems.

Radio Host   That's right, she left you a book of poems?

Stuart   Yes, and so David helped me set some of them to music. We've released an album on his website, all the money goes to the Make a Wish Foundation.

Radio Host   And I understand it was her dream to get on Radio 2?

Stuart   I don't think she'd put it quite like that; but she did have important things to say and so I'd like to share them with you.

Radio Host   And what are you going to play for us?

Stuart   This is a poem she wrote the day before she died . . . It's called 'Missing the Moon'.

Radio Host   Over to you, Stuart.

Stuart   Thank you. This is for you, Zara.

Stuart *takes a deep breath.*

There is a long pause.

He plays 'Missing the Moon' on the guitar. The song can be sung by **Stuart** *alone, or split between* **Stuart** *and* **Zara**.

We should have known
Things could get better
Maybe on paper
We should have known
We should have known
People are people
Careless in courage
But scared to the bone
And I may go gentle into this good night
For rage isn't where my ley lines lie.
We should have known
I'm not a temple
But no less deserving
Of bringing to bloom
And I have learned
There's no great secret

I'm not a planet
Missing the moon
And I may go gentle into this good night
For rage isn't where my ley lines lie
And when there's no dignity left in the fight
I'm heading straight into the light
And there's comfort in love
When you know you'll never give it up
But when it comes to being loved
I've got to learn when to give it up
We should've known.
Peace is no failure
And that's no disservice
To all that we've done
And I have learned
There's no big future
and of all the people
I'm only one
So I may go gentle into this good night
For rage isn't where my ley lines lie
And when there's no dignity left in the fight
I'm heading straight into the light
And I may go gentle into this good night
For rage isn't where my ley lines lie
And when there's no dignity left in the fight
I'm heading straight into the light

The song ends the play. Lights fade down.

The End.

Discover. Read. Listen. Watch.

A NEW WAY TO ENGAGE WITH PLAYS

This award-winning digital library features over 3,000 playtexts, 400 audio plays, 300 hours of video and 360 scholarly books.

Playtexts published by Methuen Drama, The Arden Shakespeare, Faber & Faber, Playwrights Canada Press, Aurora Metro Books and Nick Hern Books.

Audio Plays from L.A. Theatre Works featuring classic and modern works from the oeuvres of leading American playwrights.

Video collections including films of live performances from the RSC, The Globe and The National Theatre, as well as acting masterclasses and BBC feature films and documentaries.

FIND OUT MORE:
www.dramaonlinelibrary.com • @dramaonlinelib

Methuen Drama Student Editions

Alan Ayckbourn *Confusions* • **Mike Bartlett** *Earthquakes in London*
• **Aphra Behn** *The Rover* • **Alice Birch** *Revolt. She Said. Revolt Again*
• **Edward Bond** *Lear* • *Saved* • **Bertolt Brecht** *The Caucasian Chalk Circle*
• *Fear and Misery in the Third Reich* • *The Good Person of Szechwan* • *Life of
Galileo* • *Mother Courage and her Children* • *The Resistible Rise of Arturo Ui*
• *The Threepenny Opera* • **Jon Brittain** *Rotterdam* • **Georg Büchner** *Woyzeck*
• **Anton Chekhov** *The Cherry Orchard* • *The Seagull* • *Three Sisters* • *Uncle
Vanya* • **Caryl Churchill** *Serious Money* • *Top Girls* • **Shelagh Delaney** *A Taste
of Honey* • **Inua Ellams** *Barber Shop Chronicles* • **Euripides** *Elektra* • *Medea*
• **Dario Fo** *Accidental Death of an Anarchist* • **Michael Frayn** *Copenhagen*
• **John Galsworthy** *Strife* • **Nikolai Gogol** *The Government Inspector*
• **Carlo Goldoni** *A Servant to Two Masters* • **James Graham** *This House*
• **Tanika Gupta** *The Empress* • **Katori Hall** *The Mountaintop* • **Lorraine
Hansberry** *A Raisin in the Sun* • **Robert Holman** *Across Oka* • **Henrik Ibsen**
A Doll's House • *Ghosts* • *Hedda Gabler* • **Sarah Kane** *4.48 Psychosis*
• *Blasted* • **Charlotte Keatley** *My Mother Said I Never Should* • **Dennis Kelly**
DNA • **Bernard Kops** *Dreams of Anne Frank* • **Federico García Lorca** *Blood
Wedding* • *Doña Rosita the Spinster* (bilingual edition) • *The House of Bernarda
Alba* (bilingual edition) • *Yerma* (bilingual edition) • **David Mamet** *Glengarry
Glen Ross* • *Oleanna* • **Patrick Marber** *Closer* • **John Marston** *The Malcontent*
• **Martin McDonagh** *The Lieutenant of Inishmore* • *The Lonesome West* • *The
Beauty Queen of Leenane* • *The Cripple of Inishmaan* • **Alistair McDowall**
Pomona • **John McGrath** *The Cheviot, the Stag and the Black, Black Oil*
• **Arthur Miller** *All My Sons* • *The Crucible* • *A View from the Bridge*
• *Death of a Salesman* • *The Price* • *After the Fall* • *The Last Yankee* • *A Memory
of Two Mondays* • *Broken Glass* • *Incident at Vichy* • *The American Clock*
• *The Ride Down Mt. Morgan* • **Joe Orton** *Loot* • **Joe Penhall** *Blue/Orange*
• **Luigi Pirandello** *Six Characters in Search of an Author* • **Lucy Prebble**
Enron • **Mark Ravenhill** *Shopping and F***ing* • **Reginald Rose** *Twelve
Angry Men* • **Willy Russell** *Blood Brothers* • *Educating Rita* • **Lemn Sissay**
Benjamin Zephaniah's *Refugee Boy* • **Sophocles** *Antigone* • *Oedipus the King*
• **Wole Soyinka** *Death and the King's Horseman* • **Simon Stephens** *Punk
Rock* • *Pornography* • **Shelagh Stephenson** *The Memory of Water* • **August
Strindberg** *Miss Julie* • **J. M. Synge** *The Playboy of the Western World* • **Kae
Tempest** *Wasted* • **Theatre Workshop** *Oh What a Lovely War* • **Laura Wade**
Posh • **Frank Wedekind** *Spring Awakening* • **Timberlake Wertenbaker** *Our
Country's Good* • **Arnold Wesker** *The Merchant* • **Peter Whelan** *The Accrington
Pals* • **Oscar Wilde** *The Importance of Being Earnest* • **Roy Williams** *Sing Yer
Heart Out for the Lads* • **Tennessee Williams** *A Streetcar Named Desire* • *The
Glass Menagerie* • *Cat on a Hot Tin Roof* • *Sweet Bird of Youth*